GCSE English Literature AQA Anthology

The Study Guide

Poems from

Duffy, Armitage, pre-1914

AQA A Specification — Higher Level

This book is a step-by-step guide to becoming an expert on the Anthology part of your GCSE English Literature exam.

It's got everything you need to know — annotated poems, exam themes and worked essays.

It's ideal for use as a classroom study book or a revision guide.

What CGP is all about

Our sole aim here at CGP is to produce the highest quality books — carefully written, immaculately presented and dangerously close to being funny.

Then we work our socks off to get them out to you — at the cheapest possible prices.

Contents

* *Education for Leisure* won't be in the anthology for exams from 2010 onwards.
Stealing will only be a key poem in exams from 2010 onwards.

Section Four — Themes: Ideas, Attitudes and Feelings

Section Five — Themes: Methods of Poetry

Section Six — How to Answer the Question

☆ = Key poems as suggested by AQA

Published by Coordination Group Publications Ltd.

Editors:
Charley Darbishire, Kate Houghton, Kate Redmond, Katherine Reed, Edward Robinson.

Contributors:
Margaret Giordmaine, Roland Haynes, Shelagh Moore, Elisabeth Sanderson, Nicola Woodfin.

With thanks to Kate Houghton, Jennifer Underwood and Paula Barnett for the proofreading.

ISBN: 978 1 84146 892 1

Groovy website: www.cgpbooks.co.uk

Jolly bits of clipart from CorelDRAW®
Printed by Elanders Hindson Ltd, Newcastle upon Tyne.

How To Use This Book

This book will help you to do better in your GCSE English Literature Anthology Exam. It's full of straightforward ways of getting extra marks. Start by asking your teacher which poems and themes you need to study: some schools get you to study all of them, others pick out certain ones.

There are Six Sections in this book

Sections One, Two and Three are about the Poems

There are two pages about each poem. This is what the pages look like:

There's a nice picture of the poet and some info about their life.

Important or tricky bits of the poem are highlighted and explained.

Difficult words are defined in the poem dictionary.

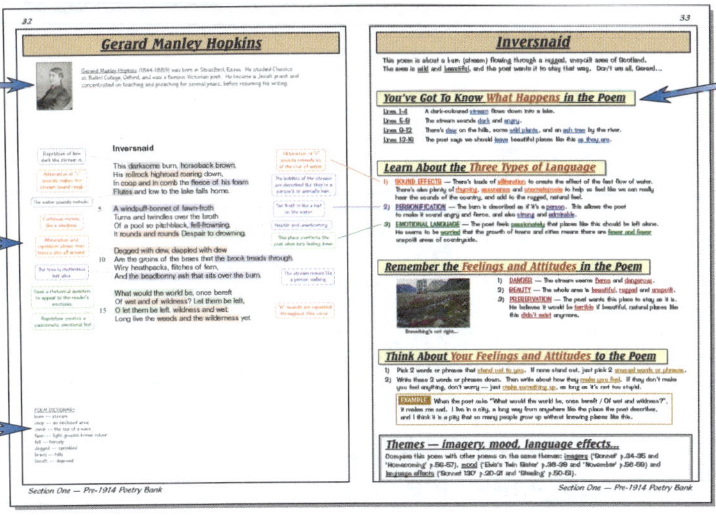

On the right-hand page there are notes about the poem. They include:

- what happens in the poem.
- the language the poet uses.
- the feelings of the poet.
- a bit that'll help you write about your personal response to the poem.

Read through the pages on the poems you've been told to study. When you've read about each poem, shut the book and write out as much as you can remember. See what you've left out, then do it again.

Sections Four and Five are about the Themes

In the exam, you'll have to compare how four poems relate to one of the themes. In Sections Four and Five, there's a page about each of the main themes that might come up. The pages tell you which poems use each theme and how different poets treat the same theme. Read them, understand them and learn them.

Section Six is about Preparing for your Exam

Pages 84-85 tell you how to plan and write good essays using CGP's 5-step method. The section also includes sample exam questions with 'A' grade answers.

Sample exam question.

A sample plan for how you could answer the exam question.

A sample student answer, which continues on the opposite page.

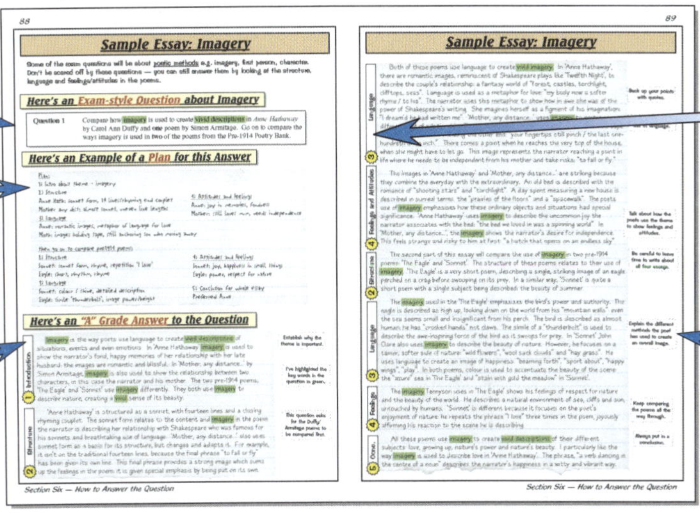

These labels show you how the answer fits into the 5-step method.

The little boxes at the side are tips on how you can get extra marks in the exam.

Write some essays using the 5-step method. Use the exam-style questions in the CGP Duffy and Armitage Anthology Workbook, if you have it, or ask your teacher for some practice questions. You get one hour to answer the question in the exam, so practise doing some timed essays.

Key Poem

Ben Jonson

Ben Jonson (1572-1637) was the son of a clergyman. He attended Westminster School, before becoming a bricklayer and later joining the army. He went on to become one of the most important poets of his time. He also wrote plays and was a friend of William Shakespeare.

The poem is written directly to his son. It's his way of saying a fond goodbye.

His "sinne" was hoping that his son would live for a long time.

Suggests that he thinks that his son's death was inevitable and something he could not control.

Jonson seems to want to be dead too.

Shows his affection for his son.

His son was his greatest creation.

He decides he'll never love anyone else so dearly because he doesn't want to feel so much pain again.

On my first Sonne

Farewell, thou child of my right hand, and joy;
My sinne was too much hope of thee, lov'd boy,
Seven yeeres tho'wert lent to me, and I thee pay,
Exacted by thy fate, on the just day.
O, could I loose all father, now. For why
Will man lament the state he should envie?
To have so soone scap'd worlds, and fleshes rage,
And, if no other miserie, yet age?
Rest in soft peace, and, ask'd, say here doth lye
Ben. Jonson his best piece of poetrie.
For whose sake, hence-forth, all his vowes be such,
As what he loves may never like too much.

He loved his son very much.

Uses money as a metaphor. Jonson's son was "lent" to him for seven years and now he has to "pay" his debt through the death of his son.

Says there are advantages of being dead, e.g. you don't have to suffer pain and old age.

This type of language is usually found on a gravestone — the poem commemorates Jonson's son.

POEM DICTIONARY
sinne — an old way of spelling sin
yeeres — years
tho'wert — you were
lament — to feel sorrow or regret
scap'd — a shortened way of writing escaped
miserie — an old way of spelling misery
hence-forth — from now on

On my first Sonne

Key Poem

This is a simple poem about a father who is mourning the death of his seven year-old son. The poem is the father's way of saying goodbye to his son.

You've Got to Know What Happens in the Poem

Lines 1-4 The man says goodbye to his seven year old son who has just died.

Lines 5-8 He says he envies his son because in heaven you don't have to deal with all the horrible things that happen in life.

Lines 9-12 Ben Jonson says that his son was his best ever creation. He decides that in the future he won't love anyone as much as he loved his son so that he won't get so upset if they die.

Learn About the Three Types of Language

1) PRIDE and AFFECTION — The poet is very fond of his son. The poem is written as though he's talking directly to him. This makes it seem very personal and helps you to imagine the poet's feelings.
2) METAPHORICAL LANGUAGE — A metaphor about debt and money explains why his son died.
3) COMMENTS ABOUT DEATH — There are quite a few different ideas about death in this poem. On one hand the poet is sad that his son's dead, on the other he says that early death isn't all bad because you don't have to grow old and suffer pain.

Remember the Feelings and Attitudes in the Poem

1) GRIEF — The poet is really upset about the death of his son.
2) UNCERTAINTY — The poet wonders whether it is better to be dead than to be alive.
3) PAIN — He's so devastated by his son's death that he decides never to love anyone else as much, because he doesn't want to suffer like this again.

Think About Your Feelings and Attitudes to the Poem

1) Pick 2 words or phrases that stand out to you. If none stand out, just pick 2 unusual words or phrases.
2) Write these 2 words or phrases down. Then write about how they make you feel. If they don't make you feel anything, don't worry — just make something up, as long as it's not too stupid.

EXAMPLE I find it very touching that the poet describes his son as his "best piece of poetrie". Even though he was one of the best poets of his time, he thinks that having a son was a greater achievement than his writing.

Themes — death, parent/child relationships, love...

You can compare this poem with other poems about the same themes: death ('Tichborne's Elegy' p.14-15), parent/child relationships ('Before You Were Mine' p.44-45, 'Mother, any distance' p.52-53 and 'Kid' p.60-61), and love ('Anne Hathaway' p.40-41).

William Butler Yeats

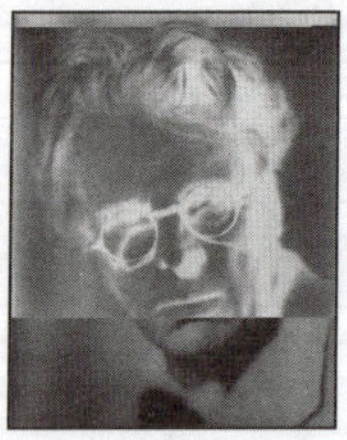

William Butler Yeats (1865-1939) was born in Dublin. He is often considered to be Ireland's greatest ever poet. As well as poetry, Yeats wrote many plays and won the Nobel Prize for Literature. He was also involved in the Celtic Revival, a movement to encourage traditional Irish culture and discourage English influences on Ireland.

The Song of the Old Mother

I rise in the dawn, and I kneel and blow
Till the seed of the fire flicker and glow;
And then I must scrub and bake and sweep
Till stars are beginning to blink and peep;
And the young lie long and dream in their bed
Of the matching of ribbons for bosom and head,
And their day goes over in idleness,
And they sigh if the wind but lift a tress:
While I must work because I am old,
And the seed of the fire gets feeble and cold.

Shows the poem is from the point of view of the old mother.

The old woman gets up really early whilst the young people lie about in bed — this is emphasised by alliteration.

Young people are only concerned by trivial matters.

The woman thinks that young people are always moaning about things that aren't important.

Suggests that the woman has no choice.

The woman gets the fire going in the morning, but by the end of the day it's going out — she'll have to do it all again the next day. This emphasises how boring and repetitive her life is.

The woman's work makes her tired and weak, just as the fire gets weaker as the day goes on.

The poem is in rhyming couplets.

List of all the rubbish jobs that the old woman has to do.

Slow, plodding rhythm suggests the boring, repetitive tasks.

Use of 'their' and 'I' emphasises the differences between the old woman and the young people.

Fire going out could be a symbol for her life coming to an end.

POEM DICTIONARY
tress — a lock of hair

The Affliction of Margaret

The poet describes the feelings of Margaret, a woman whose son has been missing for seven years. She fears the worst, and she's desperate to talk to him.

You've Got to Know What Happens in the Poem

Lines 1-14	Margaret describes the pain of not knowing where her son is.
Lines 15-21	She goes on about how good-looking and well-meaning her son was.
Lines 22-28	She says children don't realise how much their mothers worry about them.
Lines 29-42	Margaret says she was a good mother. She wants her son to return, whatever state he's in.
Lines 43-49	She says that birds have wings, so they're free to return. People don't have this freedom.
Lines 50-56	She imagines terrible things happening to her son, like being imprisoned or shipwrecked.
Lines 57-70	She says it's impossible to talk to the dead. There's no escape from her fears.
Lines 71-77	No-one can understand her grief. Her son returning to her is the only way to end it.

Learn About the Three Types of Language

1) OBSESSIVE LANGUAGE — Thoughts of Margaret's son have completely taken over her life. Her thoughts are illogical, and she feels she can't be happy about anything while her son's still missing.
2) PAIN and FEAR — She seems to torture herself by thinking of all the awful things that might have happened to him. She feels that it would be better to know he was dead than not to know anything.
3) REFLECTIVE LANGUAGE — She's sometimes more reasoning, trying to find answers. She feels she can't explain her feelings to anyone — she's alone with her sorrow, and desperate just to talk to her son.

Remember the Feelings and Attitudes in the Poem

"I hope he's got some clean underpants..."

1) SYMPATHY — The poet feels sorry for Margaret.
2) ANXIETY — He shows how anxious she is to find out how her son is.
3) DESPERATION — She feels absolutely desperate — nothing matters to her but her son.

Margaret's quite irrational at times — she tries to talk to him even though he's not there, and her mind jumps from one thought to another fairly randomly.

Think About Your Feelings and Attitudes to the Poem

1) Pick 2 words or phrases that stand out to you. If none stand out, just pick 2 unusual words or phrases.
2) Write these 2 words or phrases down. Then write about how they make you feel. If they don't make you feel anything, don't worry — just make something up, as long as it's not too stupid.

EXAMPLE The phrase "I've wet my path with tears like dew" makes me feel great sorrow for the mother. It seems there is no end to her suffering, and her pain follows her wherever she goes.

Themes — parent/child relationships, strong emotions...

You could compare 'The Affliction of Margaret' with other poems about the same themes: parent/child relationships ('On my first Sonne' p.6-7 and 'Mother, any distance' p.52-53) and strong emotions ('Havisham' p.36-37 and 'Kid' p.60-61).

William Blake

William Blake (1757-1827) was born in London and educated at home by his mother. He was a poet, artist, engraver and publisher. He believed in the power of the imagination and religion over materialism.

The lost child could be a metaphor for someone who's lost their faith.

The Little Boy Lost

The boy calls after his dad, but "father" could also mean God.

He's lost and can't see his way without God to guide him.

'Father, father, where are you going?
Oh do not walk so fast!
Speak, father, speak to your little boy
Or else I shall be lost.'

The boy sounds desperate and helpless.

The night was dark, no father was there,
The child was wet with dew;
The mire was deep, and the child did weep,
And away the vapour flew.

The child seems doomed on his own.

Could be some kind of guiding light or spirit.

As well as being found, this could mean someone who's found their faith again.

The Little Boy Found

This can be interpreted in different ways. The light could be like the star that led the wise men to the baby Jesus. Or it could be a bad spirit that is leading the little boy into danger.

The little boy lost in the lonely fen,
Led by the wand'ring light,
Began to cry; but God, ever nigh,
Appeared like his father in white.

Suggests God is always there for you when you need him.

God is a much better father to the boy than his actual father.

He kissed the child, and by the hand led,
And to his mother brought,
Who in sorrow pale, through the lonely dale
Her little boy weeping sought.

God shows the boy the way home — compare this with line 5 above.

The boy's mum seems devoted and loving — unlike his dad who failed to look after him.

The mother has been crying, just like the boy.

POEM DICTIONARY
mire — mud
fen — a marshy area
nigh — near
dale — a valley in a hilly area

The Little Boy Lost and The Little Boy Found

These two poems go together to tell a sweet little tale about a little boy who gets lost... and then gets found again, with a bit of help from God. The poems have a religious message — the poet says that God will show us the way when we're lost.

You've Got to Know What Happens in the Poems

The Little Boy Lost

Lines 1-4 — A little boy calls out to his dad, asking him to wait so he doesn't get lost.

Lines 5-8 — But his dad disappears, leaving the boy lost and crying in the rain.

The Little Boy Found

Lines 1-4 — The boy's lost on his own, but luckily for him God shows up.

Lines 5-8 — God leads the boy back to his mum, who was out looking for him.

Learn About the Two Types of Language

1) EMOTIVE LANGUAGE — The poet's descriptions of the boy make him seem helpless and vulnerable. This makes the reader pity him. It also shows how he can't cope on his own.
2) RELIGIOUS LANGUAGE — There's lots of Christian imagery in the poem. This supports the overall religious message — that we are lost without God, and can only find safety with his help.

Remember the Feelings and Attitudes in the Poems

These two poems are a bit boring, so here's a picture of something more exciting.

1) FEAR — The boy is desperate and scared.
2) CONCERN — His mother is worried sick about her son.
3) RELIGION — The poet believes people are only safe when they're with God. He thinks people are lost without God.

Think About Your Feelings and Attitudes to the Poems

1) Pick 2 words or phrases that stand out to you. If none stand out, just pick 2 unusual words or phrases.
2) Write these 2 words or phrases down. Then write about how they make you feel. If they don't make you feel anything, don't worry — just make something up, as long as it's not too stupid.

EXAMPLE When the child says "Speak, father, speak to your little boy", I feel really sorry for him. He seems completely helpless and unable to survive on his own.

Themes — danger, strong emotions, imagery...

Compare this poem with other poems on the same themes: danger ('Stealing' p.50-51 and 'Hitcher' p.66-67), strong emotions ('The Affliction of Margaret' p.10-11 and 'My father thought it bloody queer' p.54-55) and imagery ('Havisham' p.36-37 and 'Mother, any distance' p.52-53).

Chidiock Tichborne

Chidiock Tichborne (c.1558-1586) was a Roman Catholic. He was part of a plot to murder Elizabeth I and replace her with the Catholic Mary Queen of Scots. The plot was discovered and Chidiock was arrested and condemned to death. He wrote this poem in a letter to his wife, Agnes, just before his death. He was hung, drawn and quartered in 1586, at the age of 28.

Tichborne's Elegy

Written with his own hand in the Tower before his execution

My prime of youth is but a frost of cares,
My feast of joy is but a dish of pain;
My crop of corn is but a field of tares,
And all my good is but vain hope of gain.
The day is past, and yet I saw no sun;
And now I live, and now my life is done.

My tale was heard, and yet it was not told,
My fruit is fallen, and yet my leaves are green;
My youth is spent, and yet I am not old,
I saw the world, and yet I was not seen.
My thread is cut, and yet it is not spun;
And now I live, and now my life is done.

I sought my death, and found it in my womb,
I looked for life and saw it was a shade;
I trod the earth, and knew it was my tomb,
And now I die, and now I was but made.
My glass is full, and now my glass is run;
And now I live, and now my life is done.

This is supposed to be the best bit of his life.

All these lines are phrased in the same way.

He might be referring to his trial, or to the story of his life.

The fallen fruit represents his death, the green leaves represent his youth.

Nearly every word in the poem has just one syllable, making it sound plain and direct.

He probably means an hourglass (he's running out of time).

Gloomy language.

The day represents life, the sun represents enjoyment of life.

This line is repeated at the end of the other two verses as well.

The repetition of "and yet" emphasises the irony of his situation — his life's over, and yet he's still young.

The lines in this verse sound like riddles.

Contrast: end of life and beginning of life.

Very foreboding language — he's convinced he's going to die.

The poem has a regular rhyme scheme.

He hasn't got any hope.

POEM DICTIONARY
elegy — a song or verse commemorating a dead person
tares — weeds
shade — old-fashioned word for a ghost

Tichborne's Elegy

Chidiock Tichborne was about to be executed when he wrote this poem. Unsurprisingly, he's not too chuffed about the idea of dying. Little did he know that he would find everlasting life, in the pages of the GCSE AQA English Literature Anthology...

You've Got to Know What Happens in the Poem

Lines 1-6 — Tichborne contrasts his health and youth with the fact that he's about to die. He uses a series of metaphors to represent his situation.

Lines 7-12 — Another verse on the same theme, also using metaphors.

Lines 13-18 — This verse is similar to the other two, but this one mentions death directly. All three verses end with the same line, which sums up his predicament: "And now I live, and now my life is done."

Learn About the Three Types of Language

1) METAPHORICAL LANGUAGE — Tichborne uses a series of metaphors throughout the poem to make the point that he's really young and healthy, and yet his life's over anyway.
2) REPETITIVE LANGUAGE — The poem is structured in a repetitive way, e.g. each verse ends with the same line. This emphasises his main point — that he's still young, but is about to die.
3) LANGUAGE ABOUT DEATH — Death is the main theme of the poem. There's lots of miserable language and imagery about death.

Remember the Feelings and Attitudes in the Poem

1) INJUSTICE — He thinks it's unfair that he should have to die so young — he's being cut off in his prime.
2) REGRET — He feels sad that's he's got to leave life so soon.
3) BITTERNESS — There's a tiny bit of bitterness about his situation.
4) IRONY — It seems ironic to Tichborne that he's about to die even though he's young and he feels healthy.

Think About Your Feelings and Attitudes to the Poem

1) Pick 2 words or phrases that stand out to you. If none stand out, just pick 2 unusual words or phrases.
2) Write these 2 words or phrases down. Then write about how they make you feel. If they don't make you feel anything, don't worry — just make something up, as long as it's not too stupid.

EXAMPLE I find the line "And now I live, and now my life is done" very moving. The poet's clear awareness of the hopelessness of his situation is tragic. Many people in that situation might be desperately hoping for escape and freedom, but Tichborne faces his fate. I think this is brave.

Themes — death, irony and mood...

You could compare 'Tichborne's Elegy' with other poems on the same theme: death ('November' p.58-59 and 'Hitcher' p.66-67), irony ('The Man He Killed' p.16-17 and 'Salome' p.42-43) and mood ('Sonnet' p.34-35 and 'I've made out a will' p.64-65).

Thomas Hardy

Thomas Hardy (1840-1928) was born in Dorset. He trained as an architect before becoming a very well-known novelist. He wrote classic and often controversial books like 'Jude the Obscure' and 'Far from the Madding Crowd', as well as writing poetry.

The Man He Killed

'Had he and I but met
By some old ancient inn,
We should have sat us down to wet
Right many a nipperkin!

'But ranged as infantry,
And staring face to face,
I shot at him as he at me,
And killed him in his place.

'I shot him dead because –
Because he was my foe,
Just so: my foe of course he was;
That's clear enough; although

'He thought he'd 'list, perhaps,
Off-hand like – just as I –
Was out of work – had sold his traps –
No other reason why.

'Yes; quaint and curious war is!
You shoot a fellow down
You'd treat if met where any bar is,
Or help to half-a-crown.'

The whole poem's in speech marks — to make you imagine someone speaking out loud.

The 1st and 3rd lines, and 2nd and 4th lines rhyme all the way through.

Informal, friendly language — contrasts with the description of the battle in the second verse.

Very simple, straightforward description of dramatic event.

Repetition of 'because' shows he's stumbling to think of a reason why he killed the man.

He tries to reassure himself that he was right to kill the man.

Shortened, colloquial version of "enlist" (to join the army).

Informal language.

The soldier imagines that the man he killed was similar to himself.

The man he killed probably wasn't evil or nasty — just an unemployed man who joined up because he needed a job.

This line is worded almost like it's a joke — but there's a lot of bitterness in it.

Implies that everyone would do the same thing in a battle situation.

Sounds more like a friend than an enemy.

POEM DICTIONARY
nipperkin — a small amount of beer or liquor
infantry — foot soldiers
foe — enemy
traps — belongings
help to — lend
half-a-crown — old British coin

The Man He Killed

In this poem, a soldier tells us about a man he killed in battle. He says that even though the man was on the opposing side, he was probably just a nice, ordinary bloke. He reckons that if he'd met the man in a pub, instead of the battlefield, they might have been friends.

You've Got to Know What Happens in the Poem

Lines 1-4 — The soldier says that he could have been friends with the other man, if they had met in an inn.

Lines 5-8 — But they met in battle, and shot at each other. The other man was killed.

Lines 9-12 — The only reason he killed the other man was that they were on different sides.

Lines 13-16 — He imagines that the man he killed may have been very similar to him — only enlisting in the army because he needed work.

Lines 17-20 — He sums up the message of the poem. He says that war is a strange business — you kill people you might have been friends with in different circumstances.

Learn About the Three Types of Language

1) COLLOQUIAL LANGUAGE — This means informal language that sounds like everyday speech. The poem is written as if the soldier is speaking to the reader.

2) MATTER-OF-FACT LANGUAGE — The soldier uses fairly matter-of-fact, down-to-earth language to describe killing the man. This detached language contrasts with the serious message behind the poem, and helps to highlight the soldier's feeling of bitterness.

3) THOUGHTFUL LANGUAGE — The soldier thinks quite deeply about what he has done. He empathises with the man he killed.

Remember the Feelings and Attitudes in the Poem

Make beer, not war.

1) IRONY — The soldier has a sense of irony about the situation — he's killed a man who he might have been friends with in different circumstances.

2) PUZZLEMENT — It troubles the soldier that the man he killed was probably quite like himself.

3) TRAGEDY — The poet's making a point about the tragedy of war.

Writing the poem from the point of view of an ordinary soldier increases the impact of the anti-war message.

Think About Your Feelings and Attitudes to the Poem

1) Pick 2 words or phrases that stand out to you. If none stand out, just pick 2 unusual words or phrases.

2) Write these 2 words or phrases down. Then write about how they make you feel. If they don't make you feel anything, don't worry — just make something up, as long as it's not too stupid.

EXAMPLE The line "Yes; quaint and curious war is!" stands out to me because it's like an emotional outburst. All the way through the poem, the narrator sounds very restrained and matter-of-fact, and then suddenly there is this bitter, sarcastic statement. I can imagine the soldier spitting the words out.

Themes — death, irony and first person...

You can compare 'The Man He Killed' with other poems on the same themes: death ('Salome' p.42-43 and 'Education for Leisure' p.48-49), irony ('Tichborne's Elegy' p.14-15) and use of first person ('Ulysses' p.26-27 and 'Those bastards in their mansions' p.62-63).

Walt Whitman

Walt Whitman (1819-1892) was an American poet born in New York. He was one of America's earliest great poets, and was also a teacher and journalist.

Repeated to create a definite first impression of the storm.

An evil sound — dramatic and evil atmosphere.

The poem is one long sentence, with every line ending in "-ing" — this creates a sense of the storm happening right now, going on and on and on.

Patrolling Barnegat

Wild, wild the storm, and the sea high running,
Steady the roar of the gale, with incessant undertone muttering,
Shouts of demoniac laughter fitfully piercing and pealing,
Waves, air, midnight, their savagest trinity lashing,
Out in the shadows there milk-white combs careering,
On beachy slush and sand spirts of snow fierce slanting,
Where through the murk the easterly death-wind breasting,
Through cutting swirl and spray watchful and firm advancing,
(That in the distance! is that a wreck? is the red signal flaring?)
Slush and sand of the beach tireless till daylight wending,
Steadily, slowly, through hoarse roar never remitting,
Along the midnight edge by those milk-white combs careering,
A group of dim, weird forms, struggling, the night confronting,
That savage trinity warily watching.

Onomatopoeic description of the sea.

Alliteration of "s" suggests the sounds of the waves of the ocean.

Makes the elements sound like an attacking force.

Sharp and dangerous, like a sword.

The patrollers fear the worst.

Sounds deep, rough and powerful.

A defensive force, protecting the land from the storm.

The people in the patrol are hard to see in the confusion and chaos of the storm.

Like sentries on look-out.

Alliteration here sounds like the waves crashing down.

The patrollers face up to the enemy (the storm).

POEM DICTIONARY
Barnegat — a bay in New Jersey, USA
incessant — never-ending
demoniac — like the devil
pealing — making a long, loud sound
trinity — three things joined together
combs — the tops of waves
careering — moving quickly
breasting — facing, standing square-on
wending — travelling
remitting — stopping

Patrolling Barnegat

The poet describes a fierce storm blowing at night into a bay in America. Some people are patrolling the beach, standing up to the wild, cold wind. Brrrrrr....

You've Got to Know What Happens in the Poem

Lines 1-6 — A big storm is raging on a beach at night. Strong winds make massive waves in the sea which batter the land.

Lines 7-14 — Amid the dark and bleak night, people patrol the beach, facing up to the storm. They wonder if they can see a shipwreck in the distance (line 9).

Learn About the Two Types of Language

1) WAR-LIKE LANGUAGE — The storm is like a battleground between land and sea. The people on patrol on the beach are there to protect the land from attack.
2) SOUNDS OF THE STORM — There's lots of alliteration and onomatopoeia (words which sound like what they're describing). The poet uses these to create a sense of the sounds of the howling wind and roaring waves.

Remember the Feelings and Attitudes in the Poem

1) RESPECT — The poet respects the power of the storm.
2) ADMIRATION — He admires the bravery of the people patrolling the beach.
3) WARINESS — The people patrolling the beach are cautious (line 14).

There's a sense of dread surrounding the storm — the storm seems capable of great destruction.

Think About Your Feelings and Attitudes to the Poem

1) Pick 2 words or phrases that stand out to you. If none stand out, just pick 2 unusual words or phrases.
2) Write these 2 words or phrases down. Then write about how they make you feel. If they don't make you feel anything, don't worry — just make something up, as long as it's not too stupid.

EXAMPLE The description of the storm as a "savage trinity" fills me with fear. It sounds like a wild animal, with the three forces of the waves, air and night wildly attacking the land.

Themes — mood, danger and language effects...

Compare 'Patrolling Barnegat' with other poems on the same themes: mood ('We Remember Your Childhood Well' p.46-47), danger ('Stealing' p.50-51 and 'Those bastards in their mansions' p.62-63) and language effects ('The Eagle' p.24-25 and 'Inversnaid' p.32-33).

Key Poem

William Shakespeare

William Shakespeare (1564-1616) was a successful playwright and poet. He was born in Stratford-upon-Avon, Warwickshire, but lived in London for most of his life. He is one of the most important figures of Elizabethan literature.

Sonnet 130

My mistress' eyes are nothing like the sun;
Coral is far more red than her lips' red.
If snow be white, why then her breasts are dun;
If hairs be wires, black wires grow on her head.
I have seen roses damasked, red and white,
But no such roses see I in her cheeks;
And in some perfumes is there more delight
Than in the breath that from my mistress reeks.
I love to hear her speak, yet well I know
That music hath a far more pleasing sound.
I grant I never saw a goddess go:
My mistress when she walks treads on the ground.
And yet, by heaven, I think my love as rare
As any she belied with false compare.

Shakespeare wrote over 150 sonnets. This is the 130th.

The word "nothing" changes this line from a compliment into a criticism.

These lines start as if they're going to be traditional compliments.

These words might be found in a normal love poem.

Sounds ugly and coarse. The opposite of saying someone has hair like gold.

In most love poems, the woman would be compared favourably to these things.

Alternate lines rhyme for the first 12 lines.

This is the big turning point in the poem. He does love something about her.

This woman's real — not some romantic ideal.

He's says he's never seen a goddess, so can't compare her to one. This is a bit of a dig at traditional love poetry, where women are praised unrealistically.

The sonnet ends with a rhyming couplet.

Any woman.

The last two lines are inset, making them stand out.

This exclamation shows real feeling. He does love her after all.

POEM DICTIONARY
dun — a brownish-grey colour
damasked — damask roses are a type of sweet-smelling rose, damask is a type of embroidered fabric
reeks — breathes out, smells
belied — misrepresented, shown to be false

My Last Duchess

Key Poem

In this poem, a Duke is talking to a visitor about a portrait of his wife, who is now dead. He says he really likes the picture, but then he goes on about how she used to smile and have a laugh with everyone, and this annoyed him. We begin to suspect her death may have been a bit suspicious.

You've Got to Know What Happens in the Poem

Lines 1-5 — The Duke points out the portrait of the Duchess to a visitor. He's very proud of it.
Lines 5-13 — He says people always ask him about the passionate expression on the Duchess's face.
Lines 13-21 — The Duke says the Duchess's flirty expression wasn't reserved just for him.
Lines 21-34 — He says she smiled at everyone. He's annoyed that she treated him just like anyone else.
Lines 34-43 — He says it would have been wrong to criticise her for her behaviour.
Lines 43-47 — He acted to stop the Duchess's flirting — but, suspiciously, he doesn't say how he did this.
Lines 47-56 — The Duke and his guest walk away from the painting. The Duke reveals he's planning to get married again, this time to the daughter of a Count.

Learn About the Four Types of Language

1) JEALOUS LANGUAGE — The things the Duke says about the Duchess sound quite innocent at first. But we can read hidden meanings into them which hint at the Duke's jealousy, e.g. by saying she smiled a lot, he seems to suggest that she was a flirt, and maybe unfaithful to him.
2) SINISTER LANGUAGE — The Duke sometimes says things that make him sound a bit sinister — there's a dark side to him. We begin to suspect that he might have killed the Duchess.
3) LANGUAGE ABOUT POWER — The Duke feels the need to have power and control over the Duchess. He sees her as another of his possessions, just like his expensive paintings.
4) FORMAL LANGUAGE — The Duke talks in a polite, old-fashioned way. He sometimes uses this to cover up the fact that he says some pretty nasty and suspicious things.

Remember the Feelings and Attitudes in the Poem

"The brazen hussy..."

1) PRIDE — The Duke is very proud of his possessions and his status.
2) JEALOUSY — He couldn't stand the way the Duchess treated him no better than anyone else (lines 31-34).
3) POWER — The Duke enjoys the control he has over the painting (lines 9-10). He didn't have this power over the Duchess when she was alive.

Think About Your Feelings and Attitudes to the Poem

1) Pick 2 words or phrases that stand out to you. If none stand out, just pick 2 unusual words or phrases.
2) Write these 2 words or phrases down. Then write about how they make you feel. If they don't make you feel anything, don't worry — just make something up, as long as it's not too stupid.

EXAMPLE When the Duke says "all smiles stopped together", I'm very suspicious of the Duke. His tone suggests he was satisfied with the result of his "commands". Considering the Duchess is now dead, this seems rather sinister to me.

Themes — attitudes towards others, evil and first person...

You should compare this poem with other poems about the same themes: attitudes towards other people ('Havisham' p.36-37), evil ('The Laboratory' p.30-31 and 'Education for Leisure' p.48-49) and use of first person ('Elvis's Twin Sister' p.38-39 and 'Hitcher' p.66-67).

Alfred Tennyson

Alfred Tennyson (1809-1892) was born in Lincolnshire and later lived on the Isle of Wight and in Surrey. He studied at Trinity College, Cambridge. Tennyson was one of the great poets of the Victorian era and was Poet Laureate from 1850 to 1892.

The Eagle

He clasps the crag with crookèd hands;
Close to the sun in lonely lands,
Ring'd with the azure world, he stands.

The wrinkled sea beneath him crawls;
He watches from his mountain walls,
And like a thunderbolt he falls.

Alliteration — the harsh "c" sound emphasises the roughness of the eagle and his surroundings.

Strong, determined grip.

The poet describes the eagle as "he", not "it".

Personification — the eagle is described as an old man.

Far away and alone.

Surrounded by a vast emptiness.

He seems to be waiting.

Shows how high the eagle's position is.

The sea appears slow and tame from his perspective.

He waits for the right moment before diving — he's skilful.

Simile shows the eagle's incredible natural power and speed.

Like a house. The eagle owns the mountain.

Contrast with the end of the first verse. The two sides of the eagle are shown — first waiting, now acting.

POEM DICTIONARY
azure — blue

Ulysses

This poem is about the ancient Greek hero Ulysses. He's returned from the Trojan War to rule his home island of Ithaca as King — but he feels restless. He decides he needs to spend the rest of his life having more adventures. The poem ends with a rousing speech to his crew.

You've Got to Know What Happens in the Poem

Lines 1-5 — Ulysses has returned home. He feels frustrated and bored ruling his "savage" people.

Lines 6-32 — He decides he has to continue his adventures right up to his dying day. He remembers his past adventures and says there's no point in just sitting about — he has to get all he can out of life.

Lines 33-43 — He talks about his son, Telemachus. He says Telemachus is less adventurous, but he'll make a good ruler. Ulysses is proud of him — but he's a different kind of person from Ulysses.

Lines 44-61 — Ulysses addresses his crew before they set off on their voyage. He says that he and they may be old, but they're brave and strong men who are still capable of new achievements.

Lines 62-70 — Ulysses motivates his crew. He tells them that they're not as strong as they once were, and they may not come back alive, but they're brave men who will give their all.

Learn About the Four Types of Language

1) HEROIC LANGUAGE — Ulysses proudly describes his exciting adventures. He uses stirring, heroic language to fire up his crew before their next voyage.
2) IMAGERY — Ulysses creates some powerful images of his battles and adventures.
3) LANGUAGE ABOUT DEATH — He's well aware that he's old, and this makes him determined to get the most out of the time he has left. He mentions death several times, but he doesn't seem scared of dying.
4) LANGUAGE ABOUT FRUSTRATION — He feels bored and frustrated when he's not active.

Remember the Feelings and Attitudes in the Poem

1) BOREDOM — Ulysses feels bored by the thought of ruling his people at home. He seems scornful of them: "a savage race".
2) PRIDE — Ulysses is proud of his brave reputation and his great achievements in the past.
3) EXCITEMENT — He looks forward to the coming voyage and uses his own excitement to inspire his crew.

Think About Your Feelings and Attitudes to the Poem

1) Pick 2 words or phrases that stand out to you. If none stand out, just pick 2 unusual words or phrases.
2) Write these 2 words or phrases down. Then write about how they make you feel. If they don't make you feel anything, don't worry — just make something up, as long as it's not too stupid.

EXAMPLE I really respect Ulysses' courage when he says "my purpose holds / To sail beyond the sunset". This line shows he is determined to continue his adventures for as long as possible, and he is not afraid of death.

Themes — death, memory and getting older...

You could compare 'Ulysses' with other poems about the same themes: death ('Tichborne's Elegy p.14-15, 'The Man He Killed' p.16-17 and 'November' p.58-59), memory ('The Village Schoolmaster p.28-29) and getting older ('November' p.58-59 and 'Kid' p.60-61).

Oliver Goldsmith

Oliver Goldsmith (1728-1774) was an Irish playwright and poet. He studied at Trinity College, Dublin. He was also a translator and wrote children's books and histories.

The Village Schoolmaster

Beside yon straggling fence that skirts the way,
With blossomed furze unprofitably gay,
There, in his noisy mansion, skilled to rule,
The village master taught his little school;
A man severe he was, and stern to view,
I knew him well, and every truant knew;
Well had the boding tremblers learned to trace
The day's disasters in his morning face;
Full well they laughed, with counterfeited glee,
At all his jokes, for many a joke had he:
Full well the busy whisper, circling round,
Conveyed the dismal tidings when he frowned;
Yet he was kind, or, if severe in aught,
The love he bore to learning was in fault;
The village all declared how much he knew;
'Twas certain he could write, and cipher too;
Lands he could measure, terms and tides presage,
And even the story ran that he could gauge.
In arguing, too, the parson owned his skill,
For, even though vanquished, he could argue still;
While words of learned length and thundering sound
Amazed the gazing rustics ranged around;
And still they gazed, and still the wonder grew
That one small head could carry all he knew.

Rugged images of the countryside.

There are rhyming couplets all the way through.

Describing the school like this shows he was in charge.

It doesn't sound like he was much fun.

The children were frightened of him.

He took his bad moods out on other people.

The pupils pretended to find his jokes funny to keep him in a good mood.

Sounds like they were scared of his temper.

If he was severe, it was because he was so studious.

He had an impressive range of skills.

There were rumours about him, which implies no-one knew him all that well.

He was stubborn — he'd carry on arguing even when he was wrong.

Suggests he had a loud voice.

This could mean they were in awe of his intelligence, but the tone suggests they were just puzzled by him.

He was an outsider. The villagers didn't know what to make of him.

Fairly disrespectful way of describing the schoolmaster — the adults weren't scared of him.

He was very knowledgeable.

POEM DICTIONARY
furze — gorse bush
boding — predicting
counterfeited — faked
aught — anything
cipher — count, do arithmetic
presage — forecast
gauge — measure
rustics — people who live in the countryside